CASHMERE

A Guide to Scottish Luxury

LYNNE McCROSSAN

Luath Press Limited

EDINBURGH

www.luath.co.uk

Acknowledgements

To the teams at Barrie Knitwear, Begg & Co, Bute Fabrics, DC Dalgliesh, Johnstons of Elgin, Lochcarron of Scotland, Pringle of Scotland and William Lockie for imagery, access, all the lovely interviews and memories.

Brian Sweeney for shooting the capsule collection and incredible front cover – you never fail to amazing me with your talents.

To the best make-up artist on planet earth Ms Molly Jane Sheridan. You are a beautiful soul, thank you.

To the models, Charles, Georgia, Linda and Milia. Thank you for making heritage jumpers look so contemporary.

To Gabriel, thank you for going to bed on time so that mummy could write this while you were sleeping.

The team at Luath, thanks for digging deep and understanding the vision.

Muma, thanks for helping me juggle everything.

To the best bunch of girlfriends a gal could ask for, thank you for supporting me – not just while I was writing this book but over years of friendship.

And last but certainly by no means least, to the Wizard of Oz, your passion, drive and determination inspires me daily. Thank you for showing me there is no place like home.

First published 2016

ISBN: 978-1-910745-56-4 paperback
ISBN: 978-1-910745-81-6 hardback

The paper used in this book is recyclable. It is made from low chlorine pulps produced in a low energy, low emissions manner from renewable forests.

Printed and bound by
Charlesworth Press, Wakefield

Typeset in 11 point Sabon by 3btype.com

The author's right to be identified as author of this work under the Copyright, Designs and Patents Act 1988 has been asserted.

Introduction

Mills

Capsules

The Tactile Love Affair...

You never forget your first time.

It was a crisp winter's morning in the capital. The cerulean sky doing very little to trap sub-zero temperatures. Breathing looked like some smoky scene from a 1930s silent film. At the gateway to the Grassmarket stood an unassuming store with knick-knacks spilling out onto the street – the exact kind of place I feel at home shopping. Manoeuvring a multitude of items at the front door would have put off any rummaging rookie, luckily I am made of sturdier stuff and on this frosty dawn was rewarded for my fashion foraging.

Between dusty dresses and sooty books a sunbeam lead me to a jumper that on the surface looked rather retiring. Black crew neck, t-shirt shaped in nature. But as soon as I held it I knew it was different. The feeling was like nothing I had experienced before.

I was 19 years old, and in that moment a cashmere convert.

When teenage years gave way to my 20s this tactile textile became omnipresent.

As a fashion writer and stylist my quest to document all things mode meant that three seasons out of four cashmere would subconsciously find its way into my work.

Scottish heritage was something I was resistant to, mainly due to the arrogance of youth and lack of a luxury budget.

This transient relationship with trends was breeding an appreciation for artisan items without me even realising.

Editorial guidelines dictated the demographic I spoke to across print, radio and TV. It would range from high street giants, fast fashion and young designers all the way up to investment buying, established fashion houses and iconic brands.

That's when Chanel entered my orbit and everything changed.

It was December 2012 and Karl Lagerfeld was about to turn Linlithgow Place into his own personal playground, and I was granted a golden ticket to the best show in town.

The Holy Trinity

Three components collide when Scottish cashmere is created ensuring its superior softness. They are:

The Goat

The Water

The Artisan

The Glorious Goat

The story of Scottish cashmere starts thousands of miles from its bonnie shores beginning in the semi-nomadic pastorals of China and Mongolia. High in the mountains one of the world's finest treasures can be found on the backs of nimble footed goats. These incredible animals are covered with long fleece. In winter months, as temperatures tumble as low as -40 degrees, the goats grow a downy under fleece of soft short hair and it is this undercoat which is cashmere. Lightweight, yet ludicrously warm.

As spring arrives to melt away snow, the goats begin to moult. Herdsmen and their families start the painstaking task of combing the precious under fleece from their herd. The combing season lasts three to four weeks, producing small amounts per goat. It is from here that the fleece makes its way to Scotland to undertake its transformation.

It's in the Water

The marriage between Mongolian mountain goats and soft Scottish water is what makes Scottish cashmere the best in the world.

If you think about it, processing one of the finest natural fibres on the planet with incredible water can only lead to uncompromised quality. It is the same water that has made Scottish whisky inimitable. So too Scottish cashmere has become a symbol of luxury and excellence due to the country's rich natural resource. The best fibres born out of the most extreme winter conditions in Mongolia are plunged into geologically gorgeous gallons of soft Scottish water up to ten times in the cashmere process before transforming into tactile product.

Couple that with over two centuries worth of knitwear expertise and it is completely comprehensible to see why every couture house has a Scottish cashmere manufacture in their little black book.

So, although it is true you can make cashmere anywhere on earth, what makes Scottish cashmere so superior are the country's unique geographical components working together in harmony with the hair.

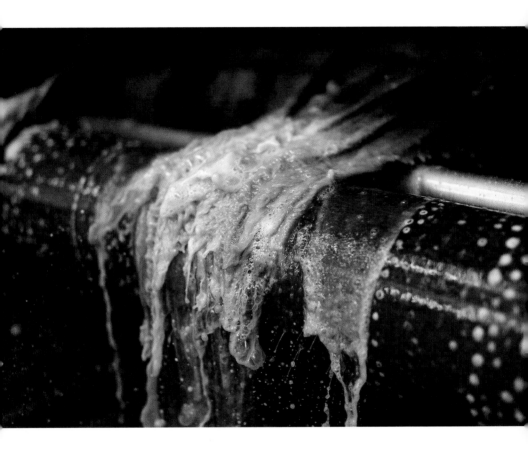

The Artisan

Since the 18th century the tradition of weaving, warping, knitting and dying have been passed down from one generation of worker to the next. Through the dizzy heights of the cashmere trade in the 19th century where over one million pieces of hosiery were being produced to times of austerity when the industry declined as cheaper cashmere flooded the market, commitment to producing luxury garments that are made to last remained at the core of the Scottish textile industry. It was that commitment that resonated with designers and customers alike as we headed into the 21st century, resurrecting the sleeping giant.

This artisanal intellectual property is woven into every ply, representing over 200 years of knowledge worth its weight in gold. Each craft person who handles the fabric is an expert in their field, many of them with over 25 years' worth of their own time invested in the processing of cashmere. All of this is felt in the finished product.

Every element elevates the quality, creating ethereal clothing with endurance.

Barrie Knitwear

WEAVING CREDENTIALS

Chanel • Hermes • Dior • Yves Saint Laurent

The story of Barrie is a modern day fairy tale. Set up in Hawick by Walter Barrie and Robert Kersel in 1903, this little mill would become the talk of the fashion world over 100 years later when a French fashion house came to its rescue.

Specialists in cashmere, Barrie and Kersel set about creating underwear for the sportier client. Their names became synonymous with top quality cashmere, producing product for Hermes, Dior and Yves Saint Laurent. In the early 1990s Chanel developed a two tone cashmere cardigan that Barrie produced for them. It was a hit, solidifying a business relationship that would safeguard a textile treasure.

In October 2012 Chanel acquired the mill after Barrie's then owner, former textile giant Dawson, went into administration, leaving the future of the Hawick factory uncertain. The marriage between mill and couture house was celebrated one wintery night in December 2012 at their annual Metiers d'Art fashion show at Linlithgow Palace.

It was a palpable performance, with the clothing, quite rightly, taking centre stage. I remember getting out of the chauffeur driven car that had whisked us from Edinburgh to Linlithgow and having my breath taken away by the attention to detail. Fire pits and lanterns led the way into the birthplace of Mary Queen of Scots where Karl Lagerfeld claimed his catwalk for the evening. The smell of rich wood burning was so evocatively Jacobean.

In that moment I felt an internal seismic shift. There was a tremendous amount of pride for a textile industry that has survived and thrived during prosperity and austerity as I watched incredible tartans, tweeds and cashmeres coming towards me. Two centuries of artisan craftsmanship being celebrated in all of its glory, with Chanel shining a spotlight on an industry that had forgotten just how magical it truly is.

Since that night Barrie hasn't looked back, but nor does it have stars in its eyes, despite supplying to the most prestigious fashion houses, including Chanel, around the world. Everything revolves around reaffirming a commitment to traditional expertise and craftsmanship. Interestingly the legendary mill still manages to find time to create its own capsule collections in-between orders. In the hands of Odile Massuger, the Ready-to-Wear collection is sculpted out of the most noble of materials while venturing outside of cashmere's usual comfort zone, adopting a modern allure at once radical and compelling.

Barrie is a symbol of excellence in an industry that is ridiculously high achieving. The standards they adhere to are echoed across Scotland, making the country the king of textiles production.

Begg & Co

WEAVING CREDENTIALS

Mulberry • Ralph Lauren • Vivienne Westwood

Cashmere comes from all four corners of Scotland. Alex Begg & Company hail from the west. In 1866 Alex Begg set up in Paisley where they made traditional, hand-woven paisley shawls that were widely used in horse-drawn carriages.

With success came the need for bigger premises, so in 1902 Begg moved an hour south of Glasgow to Ayr, to premises with new machinery which allowed for increasingly skilled weaving techniques. The key component to incredibly soft cashmere is the teaming of impeccable raw materials with rich, soft Scottish water. This is something Begg really got. The location's reliable annual rainfall is, to this day, an essential ingredient in the manufacturing process and finishing techniques that elevate their scarves and throws from very good to exceptional. To achieve that excellence gallons of the soft water which flows off the Ayrshire hills is required.

The brilliance of Begg boils down to their cross fabric ability and their knowledge of what materials go in harmony together. Their processes are still very much artisanal and hand-crafted, with traditional looms and specific machines continuing to deliver the very best results and finishes.

Much like the other mills, Begg produces product for fashion giants as well as corporate clients whilst also dedicating time developing their own lines – eight star pieces that go by the names of ARRAN, KISHORN, STAFFA, BARRA, NUANCE, TAHITI and JURA and are all woven with care.

Their signature clothe is Arran and was pioneered in 1970s. Remaining as relevant today as a winter wardrobe essential just as it was back then. Made from 100 per cent pure cashmere, Arran has a cloud-soft handle and luxurious ripple finish, achieved by the use of hand-harvested Italian teasels and their gentle brushing effect.

These spiky dried flower heads are specially grown for the company in Italy to gently brush the surface of the cashmere to raise the pile and create a characteristic ripple finish and soft handle that is synonymous with Begg. When new machinery has been proven to outperform traditional methods it has been brought in to aid the sophistication and flexibility of some lines which include over thirty different production processes.

Begg's brand, Begg & Co, was birthed in the autumn of 2013, marking the beginning of a new chapter in the company's history as it embarked on a global campaign to establish itself as a brand under a new name. It has brought a freshness and vibrancy to a 150 year old product, making it feel contemporary while retaining all of its heritage and quality.

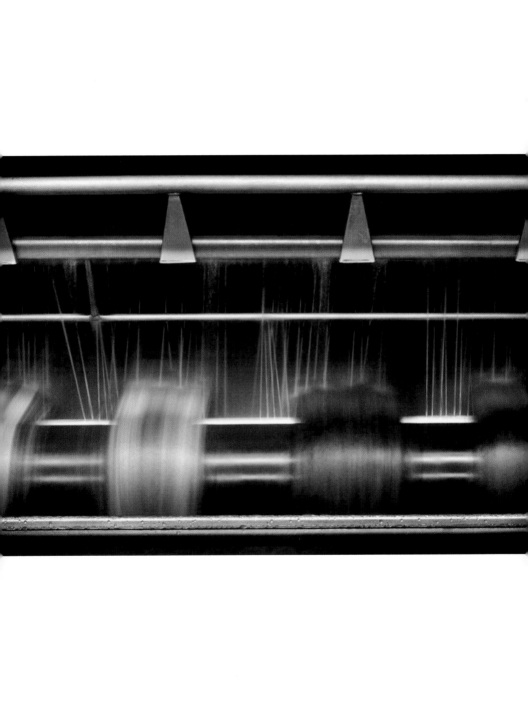

Mills

Bute Fabrics

WEAVING CREDENTIALS
Liberty • Rocco Forte, Prague
Changi VIP Lounge, Singapore
Buckingham Palace • Bank of Qatar

Walking into Bute you get the sense that the cyclical world of fashion has been delving into their archive of late to create key trends and fashion forecasts. Dig a little deeper and you realise that the Scottish textile industry possesses a certain kind of style that never dates – and that is Bute in microcosm with its dreamy Don Draper, Mad Men air and a certain '60s chic, chiselled to its core.

The story of Bute Fabric is an interesting one. It sees island and company share a unique family history, as the 5th Marquess of Bute set up the business in 1947 to provide employment for returning servicemen and servicewomen. The Bute family have been inextricably linked with the island and its development ever since. John Bute, 7th Marquess of Bute and other family members are shareholders and owners of the business to this day.

Their client list reads like a who's who in all walks of the industry, with their fabrics being used all over the globe. From Hong Kong to New York all the way back home to UK shores, Bute specialises in everything from hardwearing wool fabrics right the way up to the softest of cashmeres.

The '50s and '60s saw the mill everywhere – in glossy fashion magazines such as *Harper's Bazaar* as well as the *Buenos Aires Herald*. Even half a century ago, Bute fabric was creating outwear that wouldn't look out of place on today's catwalks, and that's testament to how well those fabrics were designed. As the fashion landscape changed so too did consumers' desire for Bute's product. The need for apparel waned while interiors took off, and, as a result of design led initiatives and collaborations, Bute became one of the UK's best known and most respected upholstery fabric manufacturers. They have worked with renowned designers such as Jasper Morrison, Tom Dixon, Barber Osgerby and Timorous Beasties. The Bute Collection has set the highest standards for the industry that keep people coming to them. In partnership with leading international furniture manufacturers, Bute has become synonymous with sophisticated contemporary textiles for hospitality, auditoria and corporate applications.

For me, Bute understand colour. This might have something to do with the cacophony they get to clock everyday while on the island. The density of their landscape is echoed inside the mill; their team has an incredible eye when it comes to blending, plus they aren't afraid to be bold and take risks. Pattern choices have a modern air to them while incorporating classic themes like herringbone and houndstooth. When you walk into their world it is the kind of place that you wish you could live. Then you rapidly realise that daydream could be reality – all you have to do is pick the fabrics and re-upholster!

INTERNATIONAL PRESS-CUTTING BUREAU
184 STRAND, LONDON, W.C.2.

Extract from

uenos Aires Herald

Argentina

Date............ **2 3 MAR 1968**

Where else can you find co-ordinate suits, sweaters, skirts, jackets and coats like these all in one department?

Where else but The Scotch House.

Coat in Bute Tweed checks £33.12.0.
Matching straight skirt £8.18.6.
Shetland Crew Neck sweater £3.15.0.

Suit in flecked Tweed pure new wool £29.8.0. Co-relating lambswool turtle neck sweater 4 gns.

Bute Tweed suit in various checks £30.19.6. Co-relating turtle neck lambswool sweater 4 gns.

Knightsbridge, London S.W.1.
Telephone: 01-589 4421
and at 84 Regent Street, London W
Telephone: 01-734 5966

FASHION
by SALLY ROWAT

COATS COME TEAMED FOR SPRING

When you buy a coat this spring you may find yourself coming away from the store with more than you bargained for. The simple explanation is that manufacturers are increasingly teaming their coats with skirts, dresses, and sometimes even culottes or trousers.

Often it's the tweeds and plain fabrics which are mixed, with stunning results—seldom, though, do qualities vary. For instance, you rarely find woollens teamed with cottons, although occasionally wool and leather or suede are made into most successful outfits.

The relatively new co-ordination in this market does mean that one no longer has the bother of searching for a coat and/or dress specifically to team with another garment. So leading fashion houses have solved at least one problem for you—on the rail—this spring.

1 "Wilton"—an elegant coat in a soft wool mixture, by Aquascutum, Street, London W1; Peter Jones, Sloane Square, London SW1; Aquascutum Bristol; Aquascutum, Lincoln; Bennett Manchester; the price ranges from approximately £39 10s.

2 Exclusive coat and dress by Tinero, in jersey with the overchecks applied by hand—in sahara/grey; black/white, cantarice or aqua/mink. Available at about 60 guineas from Patsy's Boutique at Leonards, 3 Upper Grosvenor Street, London W1; Martin's, Canterbury; Dorothy Makinson, Wilmslow, Cheshire; Huntbach, Hanley.

3 Lightweight checked coat and skirt, teamed with matching sweater by Munrospun, in lupin, lovebird, caramel, mint, or lagoon. From Roderick Tweedie Ltd at Ayr, Durham, Newcastle - upon - Tyne, Inverness, Aberdeen, Carlisle, Edinburgh; and Tissimans, Bishops Stortford—coat about £32 17s. and skirt about £8 15s.

4 This chunky herringbone tweed and leather coat, worn with tweed trousers and toning hat and sweater, was designed by a student at RCA to show fabric woven in Scotland. The tweed is by Bute Looms—the cut did not, in fact, go on to the production line, but it serves to show the outstanding effect which can be achieved by teaming trousers with a coat.

Remarkable Productivity Progress

A STRIKING rise in the productivity of the Scottish tweed industry was revealed at the annual meeting of the National Association of Scottish Woollen Manufacturers in Edinburgh. The president, Mr. Brian Dawson of Galashiels, said that though the number of weaving looms employed in the industry had declined from 2,794 in 1958 to 1,614 last year, the output of each loom had risen from 8,700 sq. yds. in 1958 to 12,840 sq. yds. ten years later.

"Taking a figure of 33½% annual growth as reasonable, the 1968 figure would have become 11,980 sq. yds. or its reaching 12,840 sq. yds. we have exceeded that rate," said Mr. Dawson. During the ten years concerned the working week had been reduced from 45 to 40 hours.

The improvement had been achieved by the introduction of new looms, the use of shift work and by the increased efficiency of the industry due to rationalisation and the result of mergers.

"When one considers the new machinery which has been installed in the yarn-making, dyeing and finishing sections of the trade, one can safely conclude that they will have progressed even more than the weaving section," said Mr. Dawson.

All the tweeds in the Bute Looms collection can be co-ordinated with plain tweeds from the colour palette of over forty shades. A preview of spring 1970 brings three new colours; Ming, a pale but deauze blue; Manilla, a warm beige; and Celadon, a minty green, all used in a collection of lighterweights and lacy open weaves.

The first Bute Looms collection of handwoven tweeds for men has also been introduced. In the main, the tweeds are designed for the export market, with Bute Looms either supplying the raw material or working with individual makers-up who are themselves concerned with export.

The bulkiest of the three cloths in the range uses a two-ply yarn in pure new wool, a top quality 7/8 oz. cloth with a soft handle. This same yarn is combined with a special new Bute Looms yarn which gives more texture to a 7 oz. cloth. The third cloth is the smoothest of the three, a 6/7 oz. cloth, pure new wool, in the new Bute Looms yarn.

Two designs from the fashion...

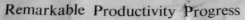

HARPER'S Bazaar

AUGUST 1958

Into

Autumn
The Suits
The Fabrics

The Young Outlook in Scotland

James Robertson Justice: SHOOTING PICNICS

Three Shillings and Sixpence

produced by the Crofton Group in conjunction with Esso Petroleum. Another article which has only just recently been granted the Design Centre Award was the clear PVC

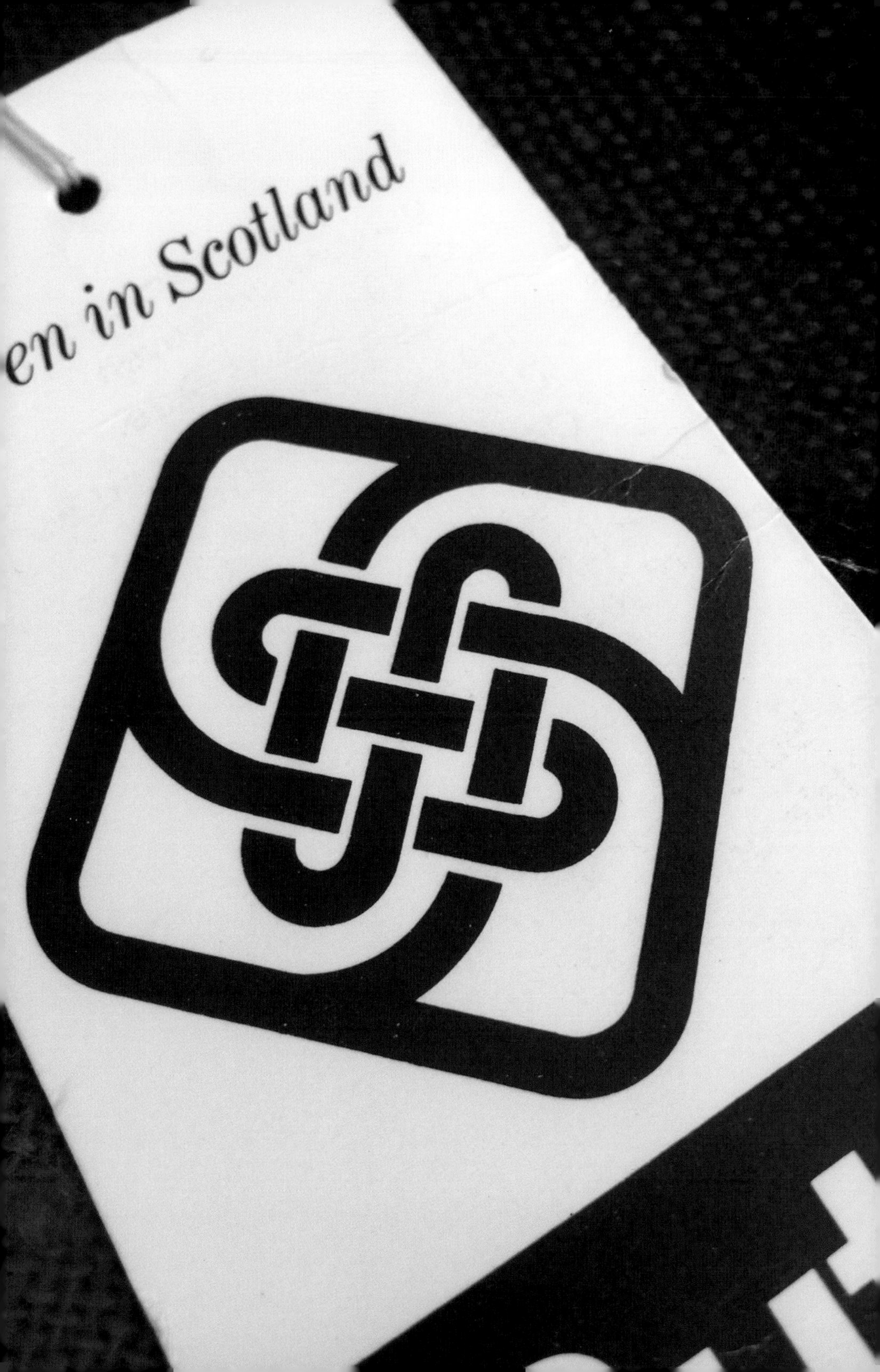
en in Scotland

DC Dalgliesh

WEAVING CREDENTIALS

Google • Pixar • Vivienne Westwood

The Dalai Lama • HRH Elizabeth II

The world's largest tartan library sits inside an unassuming mill tucked away in Selkirk shrubbery. DC Dalgliesh have been tartan specialists since the 1940s, excelling in handcrafted, single loom, artisanal heaven. They have woven more varieties of tartan than anyone else on the planet and delving into their swatch archive is how I imagine a groupie must feel being bedded by their most beloved rock star de jour.

Dixon Colton Dalgliesh first came to public prominence as a leading expert on tartans. It was this which spurred Dick into weaving for himself after running into difficulty sourcing high quality tartan fabrics that he knew were possible to create. A handful of single width looms powered entirely by pedal moved into the first incarnation of the mill.

Together with his wife, Anne, Dalgliesh ran the family business, and it blazed a trail as it grew. While Dick managed the mill back in Selkirk Anne was consumer focused, setting off several times a year for six weeks at a time to sell. She found Dick's superior fabrics an easy product to punt, and in time became a prominent business-woman in Scotland. They soon outgrew their original premises and in 1965 the family built a new mill in Selkirk, the same building that is still occupied by the weavers today. More space enabled the company to invest in double width looms, to expand the range from the single width fabrics it had produced until then.

The mill was passed to Dixon and Anne's son Kenny which he ran until 2013 before handing the reigns over to another family run Scottish company, Scotweb, in his retirement. Their aim remains to stay true to Dick's original vision of uncompromising authentic quality and out-standing customer care with 70 years of heritage behind it.

It is here the journey becomes personal. One warm autumnal day three years ago I met a man who passionatly talked about his product and dreams of bringing DC Dalgliesh into the 21st century. Nick Fiddes along with his wife Adele had a strong vision, and with me as their stylist the three of us set about showcasing incredible fabrics in a beautiful and simple way, allowing the tartan to speak for itself. Their attitudes are so in tune with the bold couple that set up the mill seven decades before them.

Moving into making cashmere from wool felt like an obvious choice when they took over, as the highest quality fabrics deserve to be woven by the experts and artisans that DC Dalgliesh have to hand. So now DC Dalgliesh combine tartan and cashmere for a truly authentic piece of fabric from their family to yours.

Johnstons of Elgin

WEAVING CREDENTIALS

Louis Vuiton • Gant • Burberry

Johnstons of Elgin are known the world over as the experts in cashmere and fine woollens, standing strong for over two centuries.

They have crammed a lot of learning in since their inception in 1797 – like the importance of building your mill next to a river that carries only the softest Scottish water, or how to weave the landscape into every one of your products. This is why keeping manufacturing on home soil is integral to their product; heritage and provenance can't be bought – it's Jonstons' values that set them apart.

Johnstons has assembled a community within the community, employing 1,000 people. At the heart of everything are the mill's workforce, each one proud of the part they play in producing impeccable products. It's not unusual for employees to reach 50 years of service, with pensioners coming back annually to celebrate with the textile institution, highlighting the love people have for the place. For 200 years two families have owned and shepherded this bastion – they are The Johnstons and The Harrisons.

One employee in particular has a special bond with the mill. Cherished childhood memories of running around gigantic ornate looms are peppered with those of clearing tables in the café at the tender age of ten, no mean feat when you have 25,000 visitors a year coming through your doors. Jenny Houldsworth, who is part of the fourth generation of family ownership of

Johnstons, is a woman holding down the ethos set by her ancestors. Having worked in a number of departments over the past decade it seems fitting that she now resides in HR, looking after learning and development much like her forefathers before her.

Here, heritage is not about nostalgia, rather it's the driving force for the future. Harnessing the wisdom gained from over 200 years in textile manufacturing ensures the company's continued prosperity. Walls steeped in history encase cutting edge technology held within, as being a family run business means true independence to adapt, evolve and innovate. Their mastery in fabrics means they can explore new horizons in luxury fabrics while continuing to create extraordinary and beautiful world class products.

Being the only vertical mill still standing in Scotland allows Johnstons to keep an unwavering eye on everything that enters and leaves the mill – from raw fibre in the wool store to perfected garment on the showroom floor, from dying to blending, carding to spinning, winding to weaving, knitting to scouring, milling to teaselling, cutting to folding, every process happens in-house. The cacophony of sounds that rise from the tireless machines is the heartbeat of the business; the vivid dyes that bubble and steam, the colours stacked from floor to ceiling. For me, the sound of the looms is synonymous with Scottish textile as a whole and the quality I see across all of the mills. Much like New York with her signature siren sound, the boom of the looms is evocative of heritage and excellence.

Lochcarron of Scotland

WEAVING CREDENTIALS

Jean Paul Gautier • Paul Smith • Calvin Klein

Comme des Garçons

If you ever find yourself in Selkirk for a reason un-textile related you would be forgiven for thinking it was a sleepy little Borders town where the pace of life hovers above slither. However, looks can be deceiving. Within this quiet, quaint, evergreen town is an efficient industry that delivers domestically and internationally.

Selkirk is home to Lochcarron of Scotland, the world's leading manufacturer of tartan. The mill was established by John Buchan in 1947, but their linage goes much deeper than that. Buchan embodied the entrepreneurial spirit many of his textiles predecessors possessed. Shortly after establishing Lochcarron, Buchan bought over another mill established in 1892, marrying the two companies together in unrivalled heritage and expertise.

'Made in Scotland' is still a proud ethos upheld at Lochcarron by skilled craftsmen and women who design, dye, warp, weave, mend and tailor tartans and textiles. A truly global brand with timeless appeal, Lochcarron offers a unique authenticity and showcases the very best of Scottish textiles. From kilt to catwalk, the mill has championed traditional tartan fabric manufacturing whilst continuing to innovate and design bespoke creations for major international fashion houses.

One of those special relationships comes from the Far East, a business partnership that Dawn Robson-Bell, Design & Sales Director, thrives on. Having been at the helm for over 25 years, all the while collaborating with iconic British high street institutions and top European couture houses, it is the Japanese market that holds a special slot in her heart. Comme des Garçons have used Lochcarron of Scotland to create their textiles for as long as Robson-Bell has been there. That kind of loyalty and longevity in fashion is a rare and unique thing.

Manufacturing for other fashion lines is part and parcel of daily life at Lochcarron but it is only one half of their story.

The mill's own range proves popular with its adoring public, and let's be honest, if it's good enough for Royalty then it's good enough for all of us. The Lochcarron of Scotland accessory collection of scarves, ties, throws and stoles perfectly combines classic tartans with super soft cashmere, lambswool and lightweight merinos. Iconic pieces are accompanied by a new range of contemporary accessories which launched in spring of 2016, including bags and small leather goods, all featuring 100 per cent wool fabrics woven in Scotland and complemented by a sophisticated seasonal colour palette.

Lochcarron do scale incredibly well, catering to the needs of big business and individual consumers on top of providing product to the high street and high end labels. They understand how heritage manufacturing and marketing cohabit in a modern world ensuring.

CLAN TARTANS

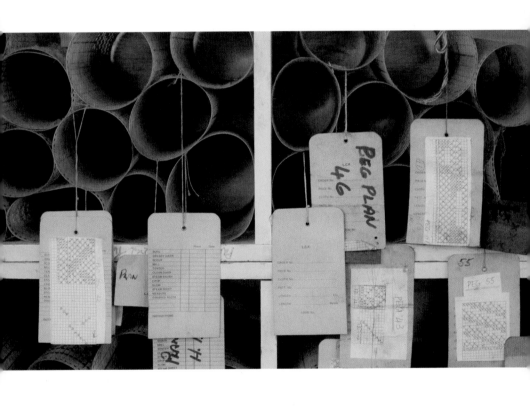

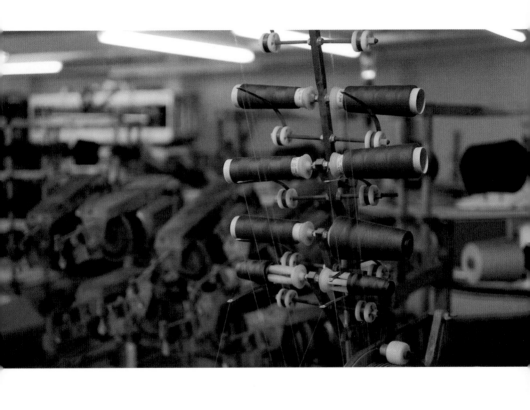

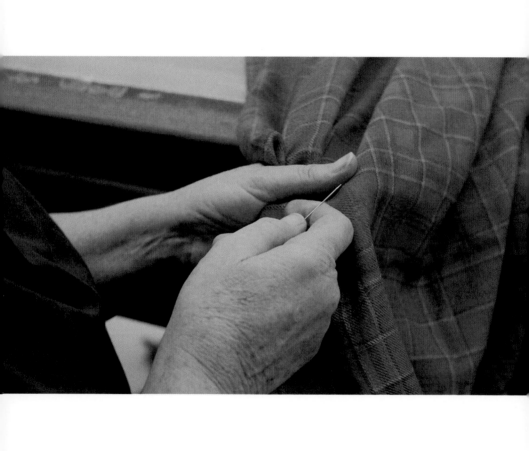

Pringle of Scotland

WEAVING CREDENTIALS

Grace Kelly • Tilda Swinton • Sophia Loren

Pringle of Scotland are the playboys of Scottish textiles. A brand that spent the last 100 years courting celebrity at the forefront of pop culture, while the 100 prior saw them crafting their skills and paving the way to becoming innovators in knitwear.

Established in 1815 by Robert Pringle, the company bearing his name didn't move into knitwear until the 1870s – and it's a good job they did, as it is here that they excel. Pringle's journey began in luxury cashmere hosiery, progressing in design with the invention of the cashmere twinset that we all know and love today. Intarsia is also accredited to the brand. Argyle designs in all things diamond shaped were dominated by them, really giving Pringle a unique look that pulled strongly on Scottish heritage. Truth be told, Argyle print had been around for a century before they made it famous – but it is the might of their marketing power that makes you think of them when you see it.

Pringle understood endorsement like no other brand in the 1950s and '60s with Hollywood starlets lining up to be dressed in the super soft finery. Grace Kelly was said to fly to New York and pick out a piece of cashmere from their store when she had something to celebrate. Her archive was unlocked in 2013 when Pringle of Scotland asked Central St Martins to collaborate on a project celebrating their iconic muse. This is where my world and Pringle really collided. Shooting the collection alongside contemporary Scottish designers was a career highlight and the catalyst that opened my eyes to how incredible our textile heritage and contemporary relevance truly is.

The 1980s and 1990s saw the brand dominate in sport sponsorship, linking with golf legends Nick Faldo and Colin Montgomery to create sportswear that ultimately did them a disservice despite its commercial success, becoming synonymous with the casual movement on football terraces across the UK. As yet another recession hit it looked like the company might face closure for good, but foreign investment saved the label as it slipped from Scottish hands into the ownership of a Hong Kong based company.

Technically there is no Pringle of Scotland mill, and only selected items come back to Scotland to allow product to carry the label stating their origin. However, other Scottish cashmere mills make some Pringle pieces and help to retain impeccable quality in its cashmere.

Pringle of Scotland is more of a label now than the other institutions who produce our iconic cashmere. Its strengths lie elsewhere, in storytelling and beautiful collaborations that leave people wanting to hear and see more. Watching them reach their milestone 200th anniversary in 2015 was a wonderful thing. The imagery they created was simply breathtaking – a wonderful way to celebrate a brand that has touched so many.

1907

VOGUE

APRIL 15

2 Summer Fashio

charted an

Tra

for a

William Lockie

WEAVING CREDENTIALS

Norton and Sons • Dolce & Gabbana

James Bond • Chanel

A parent is faced with a clothing conundrum as his five year old fidgets in her tiny lambswool cardigan.

The fabric is itchy and alien to a child embarking on a dewy education. Neither father or daughter could ever really identify the root of discomfort – be it the newness of a milestone, or fate inducing a catalyst to a career no one had envisaged.

Whatever the case, the doting dad set about creating a cashmere cardigan for his little one to wear to school. Sounds slightly ostentatious, right? Only until you discover said dad is the managing director of a company that has specialised in Scottish cashmere since 1874.

William Lockie was born in 1835, and his career began in the finishing department of a hosiery manufacturer, Messrs William Laidlaw and Sons. Lockie found himself setting up his own business at a time of industrial boom and entrepreneurial highs. The sleepy town of Hawick was transforming into an internationally renowned knitwear hub that would soon be producing over one million pairs of woollen socks a year. This growth was down to the development of mechanical knitters by Baillie John Hardie in 1771. You may be familiar with the term Luddite, but what you may not know is that this term directly comes from Hardie and his new technology, which metamorphosed Hawick, sparking the Luddite Riots between 1811 and 1816 as workers protested the advances of technology in textiles.

In the 1870s William Lockie began his business at the peak of the town's industrial power. Seizing an opportunity to buy his old workplace's equipment when Laidlaws abandoned their hosiery work, Lockie set about building a company that soon found a readymade market for his goods.

After his death in 1900 the company was passed down to his nephew, Walter Thornburn, as Lockie was never married. The mill survived the ever changing textile landscape of the 20th century, enduring recessions and buyouts and the threat of cheaper cashmere suppliers around the world flooding the marker with inferior product. Despite the overall move towards consumers buying cheaper cashmere, William Lockie stayed true to the impeccable quality that it was famous for.

And what of the little girl in her cashmere cardigan heading off to school? Well, Rachel Nuttall is now William Lockie's sales and marketing director, steering the next chapter of William Lockie's story like her father and grandfather before her. A formidable force who is watching the rebirth of an industry that has seen a lot of heartache in recent decades, her outlook is bright, mirroring her personality. Lockie's customer list reads like a who's who of designer heavyweights. Her dream is to put Lockie's name on everyone's lips.

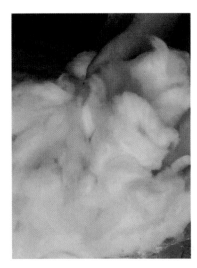

Burleigh Funnel Nec

Burleigh Crew

A Capsule Collection

Any woman worth her salt has a capsule wardrobe ready for every eventuality.

These are the go-to items that remain in your closet for decades. You will be all too familiar with them. It's the coat, suit, t-shirt, cardigan, jumper, black boots, the list goes on. In essence the staples that everything else orbits.

These are investment-worthy pieces, and stick around a lot longer than transient trend purchases.

By winding the style clock back to the beginning of the 20th century we see shopping habits that supported a capsule wardrobe right up until the late 1980s. A shift in consumerism and consumption towards fast fashion meant that investment buying became a thing of the past as the want for cheaper and newer brainwashed shoppers. This shift in attitude is a false economy and has led us to spend more money while creating a recycling crisis. Annually, we are binning around 1.4 million tonnes of clothing and textiles, worth an estimated £25 million, in the UK alone.

When you invest in something it means you are committed to it. Quality is key to these investment choices; going to the highest level of a budget you are financially comfortable with means there is longevity in your choice. Commit to good materials, great craftsmanship and classic items that won't age over passing decades.

Follow these key guidelines and the quest for unique, chic dressing will only be a few staple buys away.

My cashmere capsule collection is a no brainer. Six rotatable staples that will be with you for the rest of your life, should you chose to invest and take care of that investment.

They are:

The Houndstooth

The Argyle

The Hoodie

The Cashmere T-shirt

The Cable-knit

The Wrap

Capsule Collection

houndstooth

(*houndz-tooth*): adjective – woven or printed
with a pattern of broken or jagged checks:

a houndstooth coat.

Origins

Houndstooth goes by many different names. There's dogstooth, dogtooth, hound's tooth, hounds tooth check, puppy tooth – for smaller scale patterns (too cute) – and my personal favourite, the shepherd's plaid.

Classically it is a duotone textile characterised by broken or abstract check with four pointed corners. Mainly monochrome in colour, houndstooth has made its mark in black and white, however any colours can be used.

Its roots can be traced to the Scottish Lowlands where it was woven into wool cloth. Its fan base is broad and wide, from Sir Walter Scott and Charles Dickens to Christian Dior and Alexander McQueen.

Capsule Credentials

This print is pretty much omnipresent all year round. Working well in both winter and spring wardrobes. It is a clean, chic textile with chameleon-like qualities working in a multitude of style genres from punk to preppy.

What's so great about this print is that for almost a century true fashion diehards have been using and wearing it. I am convinced houndstooth was the real reason The Auld Alliance comes about, you only have to look at the French fashion houses to see the treaty is alive and well. Am I right Chanel, Dior et Vuitton? Oui!

Argyle

(*ahr-gahyl*): noun – A geometric knitting pattern of varicoloured diamonds in solid and outline shapes on a single background colour; also – a sock knit in this pattern a diamond-shaped pattern of two or more colours, used in knitting socks, sweaters, etc.

Origins

I am a child of the '80s, when Argyle knits adorned every golfing legend and Sunday afternoon swinger down the country club – I'm referring to the golf course, of course. This was my first introduction to a pattern that has been adopted by so many worldwide.

To be frank, the '80s gave an absolute kick-in to Argyle's fashion credentials but the passage of time has smoothed those sporting edges. In reality Argyle has always belonged the classic-set dressers – you don't get over 200 years of longevity as a pattern without style being on your side. You only have to look at the chicest dressers in the '40s and '50s to see why this print is so ubiquitous.

Being adored by so many sections of society can only be a good thing, and I urge every wearer to do this look as THEY see fit. It's fashion after all, have fun with it.

Capsule Credentials

Pop culture is littered with argyle gems. James Dean donning a beige/black concoction in *East of Eden*. Claudia Schiffer doing off-duty model chic in oversized argyle sweaters. Cher Horowitz wearing her grey and white diamond motif skirt to fail her driving test in *Clueless*. Even Paul Newman rocks it circa all of the '60s.

The modern day shift in menswear has really put argyle back on the map, both Dior and Balmain featuring it in collections. There is a lovely duality and gender neutrality about argyle that gives it durability. In short, Argyle will be in your wardrobe forever.

hoodie

(*hoo-d-ee*): noun – (informal) – a hooded
sweatshirt

Origins

You may be fooled into thinking this garment is a relative new kid on the block – that's where you'd be wrong. The origins trace back to utility wear in medieval Europe. Fast forward to the roaring '20s and the humble jumper we call hoodie undertakes its final fashion transfiguration into the garment we wear today.

Hoodie roots have remained in workwear, its felicitous nature making sportswear its natural home at the start of the 20th century. Adopted by nonconformists, this inconspicuous piece of clothing has become a complicated cultural symbol.

Capsule Credentials

This is dreamy dress down attire. Think weekend lounging, cosy, comfortable clobber that maintains a style edge. There's a reason sports luxe was coined as fashion terminology, I like to think the black cashmere hoodie was the nucleus for the movement.

The hoodie sits within its own set of rules for the wearer. Add cashmere and this congruous concoction will leave you with plenty to play with in your wardrobe.

Pop it underneath suiting to give a casual visual to workwear or plonk it on with some stretchy trousers and trainers it takes the slacker edge off slob dressing (one of my favourite vibes). Part of *The One Hundred: A Guide to the Pieces Every Stylish Woman Should Own,* the cashmere hoodie has the luxury of going with everything in your established wardrobe.

T-shirt

(*or tee-shirt, tee shirt*): noun – a lightweight, usually knitted, pullover shirt, close-fitting and with a round neckline and short sleeves, worn as an undershirt or outer garment.

Origins

The humble T is over 100 years old, beginning life as a military garment between the Spanish-American war and the early 1900s.

Its transformation into style staple circles around Pringle of Scotland's twin-set invention of the 1930s. The twin-set is part of Scotland's textile royalty, a gem that placed us on the map *a la mode* with Hollywood starlets and feverish fashion followers alike.

Two components created the look, a crew neck cashmere t-shirt sitting underneath a cardigan of the same colour.

Capsule Credentials

Lana Turner. Grace Kelly. Carole Lombard. Jean Simmons. All part of the cashmere t-sisterhood, not bad company to kick it with.

The cashmere t-shirt from this day forth shall be known as 'the all rounder'. It can take you from day to night, formal to casual and most importantly winter to summer. If you're going to own only one piece of cashmere, this is THE ONE.

Cable-knit

(*cable-knit*): adjective – having or made with
a knitting stitch that produces a pattern
resembling the twist of a usually two-ply cable;
a cable-knit sweater

Origins

During the 17th and 18th century knitwear dominated infrastructure in Scotland. Kicking off with accessories from socks and stockings, right through to underwear and jumpers. During this time Fair Isle techniques were honed and developed, leading the way to the cable stitching used on Aran sweaters.

It's in the early 20th century that we see cable-knit becoming a fashion symbol rather than practical workwear for fishermen. The post Second World War boom allowed knitwear to become flavoursome with haute couturiers and knitting crazes took off around the globe.

Capsule Credentials

There is not an autumn-winter that passes you do not see an adaptation of a cable knit go down a runway or hit the high street. Sure as the seasons change and snow follows sun, so too do these jumpers make an annual appearance. For that reason it's a no brainer to invest in one that will see you though not just one winter but several decades' worth.

Due to the dense, soft nature of goat hair the marriage between cashmere and a chunky knit means warmth is at a maximum. The better the cashmere quality the warmer you will be. The higher the ply, the softer it will feel. For me, grey makes sense. It's a natural tone, easy to keep at that shade should anything go awry in the cleaning process plus it goes with every colour, print and texture you can throw at it.

The Wrap

(*wrap*): verb – simple definition of wrap –
to cover (something) by winding or folding
a piece of material around it; noun – piece
of clothing to be wrapped or folded about a
person, especially an outer garment such as a
robe, cloak, or coat.

Origins

Our most salacious of cover-ups, the wrap's evolution is one worthy of gossip. Design power house Diane von Furstenberg claims the invention as her own, and although it is certainly synonymous with the living legend, the roots go deeper than the dawn of disco in the '70s.

We find ourselves heading further back to the '30s, when Elsa Schiaparelli was delving into Dadaism in her designs, to truly witness the conception of the wrap. This flowing frock was in essence a way of giving freedom to the female form. A symbol of sexual liberation, this item of clothing has become its own movement within a woman's wardrobe.

Capsule Credentials

As a stylist I know there is no such thing as one size fits all. Different body shapes demand different treatments when it comes to dressing. Having said that, there is always one thing that defies any rule. In this case it is the wrap. Tall, short, slim, thick, busty, bony, hippy or skinny – whatever style your mortal coil comes in a wrap will be your buddy.

You only have to look at the dedicated followers of fashion wearing wraps through the decades to see confirmation of this. From Hollywood royalty to real life Queens and Princesses, this item is loved by all. I haven't yet found a body shape this style doesn't work on. Couple style ergonomics with cashmere and you have a match made in sensual heaven.

LYNNE MCCROSSAN is a writer and stylist living in Edinburgh. For a decade she has commented on fashion across radio, TV and newspapers for the BBC, STV, *Scotland on Sunday* and the *Edinburgh Evening News* working with brands such as Chanel, Mulberry, Harvey Nichols and House of Fraser. She is also Brand Guardian of the world's only handcrafted tartan mill, DC Dalgliesh and recently establishment her own knitwear label **CROSS**CASHMERE.

This is her second book. *A Girl's Guide to Vintage* was her first.

www.crosscashmere.com